WHOLE FOOD PLANT-BASED COOKBOOK

MORE THAN 100 RECIPES DI HERBS ET PLANTS WITHOUT SALT, OIL AND REFINED SUGAR FOR HEALTHY, BALANCED LIVING

MICHAEL CARROLL

All rights reserved.

Disclaimer

The information contained in this eBook is meant to serve as a comprehensive collection of strategies that the author of this eBook has done research about. Summaries, strategies, tips and tricks are only recommendation by the author, and reading this eBook will not guarantee that one's results will exactly mirror the author's results. The author of the eBook has made all reasonable effort to provide current and accurate information for the readers of the eBook. The author and its associates will not be held liable for any unintentional error or omissions that may be found. The material in the eBook may include information by third parties. Third party materials comprise of opinions expressed by their owners. As such, the author of the eBook does not assume responsibility or liability for any third party material or opinions. Whether because of the progression of the internet, or the unforeseen changes in company policy and editorial submission guidelines, what is stated as fact at the time of this writing may become outdated or inapplicable later.

The eBook is copyright © 2022 with all rights reserved. It is illegal to redistribute, copy, or create derivative work from this eBook whole or in part. No parts of this report may be reproduced or retransmitted in any reproduced or retransmitted in any forms whatsoever without the writing expressed and signed permission from the author.

TABLE OF CONTENTS

TABLE OF CONTENTS 3

INTRODUCTION 7

HERB BLENDS 9

    1. Salt-Free Blend 10
    2. Italian Seasoning 12
    3. Garden Blend 14
    4. Poultry Herbs 16
    5. Fish Herbs 18
    6. Spicy Chicken Rub 20
    7. Pumpkin Pie Spice Blend 22
    8. Breakfast Spice Shaker 24
    9. Curry Powder 26
    10. Fajita Blend 28
    11. Seafood Spice 30
    12. Chicken Bouquet 32
    13. Beef Bouquet 34
    14. Fish Bouquet 36

HERBAL JUICES AND SMOOTHIES 38

    15. Strawberry and Macadamia Smoothie 39
    16. Goji Berry and Pine Nut Smoothie 41
    17. Blackcurrant Booster Smoothie 43
    18. Sour Cherry and Raw Cocoa Smoothie 45
    19. Almond and Rose Smoothie 47
    20. Pistachio and Avocado Smoothie 49
    21. Maca and Mango Smoothie 51
    22. Plum and Fennel Smoothie 53
    23. Power Berry Smoothie 55

24.	EARLY AUTUMN RAMBLER'S DELIGHT	57
25.	GARDEN GREENS JUICE	59
26.	RED PEPPER AND SPROUTED SEEDS JUICE	61
27.	GINGER AND FENNEL JUICE	63
28.	FENNEL AND BROCCOLI SPROUTS JUICE	65
29.	BUCKWHEAT GREENS AND PEA SHOOT JUICE	67
30.	TOMATO SALSA JUICE	69
31.	ARTICHOKE LEAF AND FENNEL JUICE	71
32.	SUNFLOWER GREENS AND WHEATGRASS JUICE	73

HERBAL TEAS 75

33.	LEMON BALM AND ROSE TEA	76
34.	JASMINE AND LEMONGRASS TEA	78
35.	GOJI BERRY AND DAMIANA TEA	80
36.	ROSEHIP AND BILBERRY TEA	82
37.	CHRYSANTHEMUM AND ELDERFLOWER TEA	84
38.	CHAMOMILE AND FENNEL TEA	86
39.	DANDELION AND BURDOCK TEA	88
40.	YARROW AND CALENDULA TEA	90
41.	SKULLCAP AND ORANGE FLOWER TEA	92
42.	BLACKBERRY AND WILD STRAWBERRY TEA	94
43.	PEPPERMINT AND CALENDULA INFUSION	96
44.	HAWTHORN FLOWER AND LAVENDER TEA	98
45.	NETTLE AND CLEAVERS TEA	100
46.	MULLEIN AND MARSHMALLOW TEA	102
47.	HORSETAIL AND CORNSILK TEA	104
48.	FRUITED HERBAL ICED TEA	106
49.	RASPBERRY HERBAL TEA	110
50.	CARDAMOM TEA	112
51.	SASSAFRAS TEA	114
52.	MORINGA TEA	116

| 53. | Sage Tea | 118 |

CORDIALS AND SYRUPS ... 120

54.	Blackberry and Lime Cordial	121
55.	Elderberry and Elderflower Cordial	123
56.	Sweet Violet and Ginger Honey	126
57.	Lemon Balm and Honey Purée	128
58.	Rosehip Syrup	130
59.	Mullein and Aniseed Syrup	132
60.	Rose Petal Syrup	134
61.	Sour Cherry Syrup	136
62.	Echinacea and Thyme Syrup	138

HERBAL TINCTURES ... 141

63.	Peppermint and Thyme Tincture	142
64.	Elderberry and Liquorice Tincture	144
65.	Lime Flower and Hawthorn Berry Tincture	147
66.	Passionflower and Chamomile Tincture	150
67.	Chaste Berry and Dang Gui Tincture	153
68.	Goji Berry and Siberian Ginseng Tincture	156
69.	Red Clover and Cleavers Tincture	159
70.	Echinacea and Elderberry Winter Guard Tincture	162
71.	Dandelion and Burdock Tincture	165
72.	Crampbark and Valerian Tincture	168
73.	Black Cohosh and Sage Tincture	171
74.	Birch Leaf and Nettle Root Tincture	174

HERBAL FOODS ... 177

75.	Crumbled Herbal Chicken	178
76.	Cream of Chicken with Herbs	181
77.	Apricot Dijon Glazed Turkey	183
78.	Chicken and Rice on Herb Sauce	186

79.	CHICKEN IN CREAM AND HERB	188
80.	CHICKEN MADEIRA ON BISCUITS	191
81.	CHICKEN SOUP WITH HERBS	193
82.	CHICKEN WITH WINE AND HERBS	196
83.	HERBAL RAVIOLI	198
84.	LINGUINE WITH MIXED HERB	201
85.	FARFALLE WITH HERB SAUCE	204
86.	EGG NOODLES WITH GARLIC	206
87.	CAPPELINI WITH HERB SPINACH	208
88.	MALAYSIAN HERBAL RICE	211
89.	ANGEL HAIR WITH SMOKED SALMON	214
90.	CODFISH WITH HERBS	217
91.	COLD POACHED SALMON	220
92.	DILL HERB FILLETS	222
93.	CRISPY BAKED FISH AND HERBS	224
94.	FETTUCCINE WITH SHRIMP	226
95.	MUSSELS WITH GARLIC	228
96.	FISH CARIBBEAN WITH WINE	231
97.	MONKFISH WITH GARLICKY HERB	234
98.	HERBED PORK CUTLETS	236
99.	MONASTERY HERBAL SAUSAGE	238
100.	FILLET OF LAMB WITH HERBS	240

CONCLUSION **242**

INTRODUCTION

There is no general rule about how much herbs to use. Most recipes specify an amount in the list of ingredients. If you don't have a recipe to follow, start with $\frac{1}{4}$ teaspoon and add more as needed to reach your ideal flavor. You don't want the herbs to overpower the other flavors in the dish.

Dried herbs are stronger than fresh herbs so you will need to use more of the fresh herbs. If the recipe calls for 1 teaspoon of dried, crushed herbs or $\frac{1}{4}$ teaspoon of powdered herbs, use 3 teaspoons (1 tablespoon) of fresh. The following dried-herb blends are great to try with any dish. Remember to adjust the amount when using fresh herbs.

Common herbs

A. **Basil**—Tomato products (juice, pasta sauces, pizza sauce), eggs, game meats, lamb, veal, rice, spaghetti, vinaigrette, soups (minestrone, pea, potato, and vegetable), beans, eggplant

B. **Thyme**—Eggs, game meats, lamb, veal, rice, poultry, barbeque sauce, fish, oysters, chowders, soups (onion, tomato, and vegetable), mushrooms, tomatoes

C. **Rosemary** – Dumplings, eggs, game meats, lamb, veal, poultry, fish, barbeque sauce, chicken, beef, soups (pea and vegetable), beans, mushrooms, potatoes, cauliflower, turnips

D. **Oregano**—Tomato dishes, beef, game meats, veal, spaghetti, clams, soups (bean, minestrone, and tomato), beans, eggplant, and mushrooms

E. **Dill**—Tomato dishes, yeast breads, eggs, coleslaw, potato salad, fish, beans, Brussels sprouts, cauliflower, cucumber, summer squash

F. **Parsley**—Salads, vegetables, pastas

G. **Sage**—Cottage cheese, game meats, pork, rice, poultry, soups (chicken, minestrone, and vegetable), stuffing

H. **Cilantro**—Mexican and Asian cooking, rice, salsa, tomatoes

I. **Mint**—Desserts, lamb, peas, fruit salads, sauces

HERB BLENDS

1. Salt-Free Blend

makes about ⅓ cup

Ingredients
- 1 tablespoon mustard powder
- 2 teaspoons parsley
- 2 teaspoons onion powder
- 2 teaspoons thyme
- 1 tablespoon garlic powder
- 2 teaspoons dill weed
- 2 teaspoons savory
- 2 teaspoons paprika
- 2 teaspoons lemon peel

Directions
a) Combine and store in an airtight container.

b) When ready to use, mix a small amount with water to form a paste.

2. Italian Seasoning

makes about 1½ cups

Ingredients

- ½ cup dried oregano
- ½ cup dried basil
- ½ cup dried rosemary
- ¼ cup dried parsley
- ½ cup dried thyme
- 1 tablespoon fennel seeds, crushed
- ¼ cup dried marjoram
- 2 tablespoons dried sage
- ¼ cup dried oregano
- 1 tablespoon hot red pepper flakes
- ¼ cup dried savory

Directions

a) Combine and store in an airtight container.

b) When ready to use, mix a small amount with water to form a paste.

3. Garden Blend

makes about 1¼ cup

Ingredients

- 2 tablespoons dried lavender leaves
- 2 tablespoons dried fennel seeds or stalks
- 3 tablespoons dried parsley
- 3 tablespoons dried basil
- 3 tablespoons dried thyme
- 3 tablespoons dried marjoram
- 3 tablespoons dried rosemary
- 3 tablespoons dried chives
- 3 tablespoons paprika
- ½ teaspoon garlic powder

Directions

a) Combine and store in an airtight container.

b) When ready to use, mix a small amount with water to form a paste.

4. Poultry Herbs

makes about ⅓ cup

Ingredients

- 2 tablespoons dried tarragon
- 1 tablespoon dried marjoram
- 1 tablespoon dried basil
- 1 tablespoon dried rosemary
- 1 teaspoon paprika
- 1 teaspoon dried lovage

Directions

a) Combine and store in an airtight container.

b) When ready to use, mix a small amount with water to form a paste.

5. Fish Herbs

makes about ½ cup

Ingredients

- 3 tablespoons dried dill weed
- 2 tablespoons dried basil
- 1 tablespoon dried tarragon
- 1 tablespoon dried lemon thyme
- 1 tablespoon dried parsley
- 1 tablespoon dried chervil
- 1 tablespoon dried chives

Directions

a) Combine and store in an airtight container.

b) When ready to use, mix a small amount with water to form a paste.

6. Spicy Chicken Rub

Ingredients

- 2 teaspoons chili powder
- 1 teaspoon ground oregano
- 1 teaspoon cilantro leaves, dried and crumbled
- 1/2 to 1 teaspoon cayenne pepper
- 1 teaspoon garlic powder
- 1/2 teaspoon freshly ground black pepper
- 1/2 teaspoon ground ginger
- 1/2 teaspoon ground cumin

Directions

c) Combine and store in an airtight container.

d) When ready to use, mix a small amount with water to form a paste.

7. Pumpkin Pie Spice Blend

Ingredients

- 1/3 cup cinnamon
- 1 tablespoon ground ginger
- 1 tablespoon nutmeg or mace
- 1 1/2 teaspoons ground cloves
- 1 1/2 teaspoons allspice

Directions

a) Combine and store in an airtight container.

b) Add 1 to 1 1/2 teaspoons of this mix to pumpkin pie filling.

8. Breakfast Spice Shaker

Ingredients

- 1 cup sugar
- 3 tablespoons cinnamon
- 1 teaspoon nutmeg or mace
- 1 teaspoon cardamom

Directions

a) Combine and store in an airtight container.

b) Sprinkle on pancakes, toast, or oatmeal.

9. Curry Powder

Ingredients

- 4 tablespoons ground coriander
- 3 tablespoons ground turmeric
- 2 tablespoons ground cumin
- 1 tablespoon freshly ground black pepper
- 1 tablespoon ground ginger
- 1 teaspoon ground fennel seeds
- 1 teaspoon chili powder
- 1/2 teaspoon cayenne pepper

Directions

a) Combine and store in an airtight container.
b) Add to chicken or egg salad or rice, or use to make meat or vegetable curry.

10. Fajita Blend

Ingredients

- 4 tablespoons chili powder
- 2 tablespoons ground cumin
- 2 teaspoons ground oregano
- 2 teaspoons garlic salt

Directions

a) Combine and store in an airtight container.

b) Sprinkle on fajita meat or stir into meatloaf or burgers for a spicy kick.

11.   Seafood Spice

Ingredients

- 2 tablespoons allspice
- 2 tablespoons celery salt
- 2 tablespoons ground mustard
- 1 tablespoon ground ginger
- 1 tablespoon paprika
- 3/4 teaspoon cayenne pepper

Directions

a) Combine and store in an airtight container.

b) Add to seafood salads and chowders, or sprinkle on fish fillets.

12.   Chicken Bouquet

Ingredients

- 1 bay leaf
- 1 tablespoon tarragon
- 1 tablespoon parsley
- 1 teaspoon rosemary
- 1 teaspoon thyme

Directions

a) Combine and store in an airtight container.

13.   Beef Bouquet

Ingredients

- 1 teaspoon black peppercorns
- 2 whole cloves
- 1 broken bay leaf
- 2 teaspoons thyme
- 2 teaspoons marjoram
- 2 teaspoons savory
- 1 tablespoon parsley
- 1/2 teaspoon crushed lovage leaves

Directions

a) Combine and store in an airtight container.

14.   Fish Bouquet

Ingredients

- 1 bay leaf
- 2 black peppercorns
- 1 teaspoon thyme
- 1 teaspoon fennel weed
- 1 teaspoon crushed lovage leaves
- 1 tablespoon parsley

Directions

a) Combine and store in an airtight container.

HERBAL JUICES AND SMOOTHIES

15. Strawberry and macadamia smoothie

Makes 4 servings

Ingredients
- 1/2 vanilla pod
- 50g (1 3/4oz) raw macadamia nuts
- pulp of 1 young medium-sized coconut
- 250g (9oz) fresh strawberries
- a little of the coconut juice (optional)

Directions

a) Slit the vanilla pod open with a sharp knife, then scrape out the seeds.

b) Place the nuts and the coconut pulp in a blender or food processor.

c) Add the strawberries and vanilla seeds. Pulse all the ingredients to give a smooth, silky texture. If the smoothie seems very thick, add enough coconut juice to give it a better texture. Pour into 4 glasses and serve.

16.   Goji berry and pine nut smoothie

Makes 2 servings

Ingredients

- 50g (1 3/4oz) almonds
- 50g (1 3/4oz) goji berries
- 20g (3/4oz) pine nuts
- 1 teaspoons linseed oil
- 2-3 leaves of fresh peppermint 350-400ml (12-14fl oz.) mineral water

Directions

a) Place all ingredients in a blender or food processor and blend with the mineral water to give a smooth silky texture.

b) If the consistency is a bit too thick, add a little more water and blend.

17. Blackcurrant booster smoothie

Makes 2 servings

Ingredients

- 50g (1 3/4oz) fresh blackcurrants (or used dried and soak first)
- 50g (1 3/4oz) roasted barley
- 4 teaspoons agave syrup
- 4 teaspoons coconut oil
- 250ml (9fl oz.) rice milk
- A little mineral water

Directions

a) Put all the ingredients except the mineral water in a blender or food processor and blend until smooth.

b) Add enough mineral water to ensure the smoothie is of a pourable consistency.

18.   Sour cherry and raw cocoa smoothie

Makes 2 servings

Ingredients

- 50g (13/4oz) sour cherries, stoned if fresh, or dried
- 300ml (10fl oz.) rice or almond milk 4 teaspoons raw or regular cocoa powder 4 teaspoons hemp seeds, shelled 4 teaspoons flaxseed oil

Directions

a) If using dried sour cherries, soak them for few hours in 150ml (5fl oz.) of mineral water.

b) Combine half the rice or almond milk with the rest of the ingredients in a blender or food processor and blend to a smooth, silky, pourable consistency. Add the rest of the milk in stages until the texture of the smoothie is to your liking.

19. Almond and rose smoothie

Makes 2 servings

Ingredients

- 50g (1 3/4oz) almonds
- 300-400ml (10-14fl oz.) mineral water 2 1/2 Tablespoons rose syrup
- 4 teaspoons almond oil
- 1 drop rose attar essential oil (optional)
- 8 damask rose petals (optional)

Directions

a) Combine half the mineral water with the rest of the ingredients in a blender or food processor and blend to a smooth, silky, pourable consistency.

b) Add the rest of the water in stages until the texture of the smoothie is to your liking.

20.   Pistachio and avocado smoothie

Makes 2 servings

Ingredients

- 50g (1 3/4oz) pistachios (plus a few for decoration)
- 1 small avocado, stoned, peeled, and quartered
- 1 teaspoons hemp seed oil
- 2 teaspoons linseed oil
- juice of 1/2 lemon
- fresh juice of 6 celery stems
- freshly ground black pepper to taste pinch of salt
- 3-4 fresh basil leaves
- a little mineral water

Directions

a) Put all the ingredients except the mineral water into a blender or food processor and blend until smooth. Add enough mineral water to ensure the smoothie is of a pourable consistency.

b) Serve in glasses, with a sprinkle of finely chopped pistachios on top of each.

21. Maca and mango smoothie

Makes 2 servings

Ingredients
- 2 large ripe mangoes
- 2 teaspoons maca root powder
- 2 teaspoons hemp seeds, shelled
- 2 teaspoons coconut oil
- juice of 1 lemon
- 4 fresh peppermint leaves
- a little mineral water (optional)

Directions
a) Place all the ingredients in a blender or food processor and blend to a smooth, silky texture.
b) Dilute with mineral water as desired, if necessary.

22. Plum and fennel smoothie

Makes 2 servings

Ingredients

- 9-10 large dark blue-skinned plums
- 1/2 teaspoons fennel seeds
- 2 Tablespoons linseeds, soaked
- 2 Tablespoons shelled hemp seeds, soaked

Directions

a) Stew the plums first: put them in a saucepan with 250ml (9fl oz.) of mineral water, add the fennel seeds, and bring to the boil. Put the lid on and simmer on a low heat for 10-12 minutes. Allow to cool.

b) Transfer to a blender or food processor, add the remaining seeds (or oils, if using) and blend to a smooth consistency.

23.   Power berry smoothie

Makes 2 servings

Ingredients

- 2 Tablespoons fresh raspberries
- 2 Tablespoons fresh blackberries
- 2 Tablespoons fresh blueberries
- 2 Tablespoons fresh blackcurrants
- 2 teaspoons acai berry powder
- 800ml lemongrass infusion, cold
- a little mineral water (optional)
- a dash of maple syrup or a pinch of stevia powder (optional)

Directions

a) Place the fresh berries and acai berry powder in a blender or food processor, add the lemongrass infusion, and blend to a smooth, silky texture.

b) If necessary, add a little mineral water to achieve a consistency you like.

24.   Early autumn rambler's delight

Makes 2 servings

Ingredients

- 3 1/2 apples, peeled, cored, and chopped
- 1/3 pear peeled, cored, and chopped
- 12 ripe elderberries, rinsed, with all stalks removed
- 20 ripe blackberries, rinsed

Directions

a) Put all the ingredients into a blender or a food processor and blend until smooth.

b) Divide between two glasses and top with elderberry and elderflower syrup to enhance the antiviral content of the smoothie.

25. Garden greens juice

Makes 2 servings

Ingredients

- 2 handfuls of kale leaves
- 2 Swiss chard leaves
- 1 large handful of spinach leaves
- 1/2 cucumber
- 1 small green courgette
- 3 stems celery
- 2 dandelion leaves (large)
- 2 stems fresh marjoram
- a dash of lemon juice (optional)

Directions

a) Wash and juice all the vegetables and herbs, and mix thoroughly. Add the lemon juice to taste if you wish or,

b) if you prefer a more powerful lemon flavour, add an eighth of a lemon (organic is preferable) and mix well until blended.

26.   Red pepper and sprouted seeds juice

Makes 2 servings

Ingredients

- 1 red pepper, deseeded and cut into quarters
- 20g (3/4oz) sprouted alfalfa seeds
- 20g (3/4oz) sprouted red clover seeds
- 10g (1/4oz) sprouted broccoli seeds
- 1/2 cucumber
- 2-3 fresh mint leaves
- 1/2 small fresh red chilli, deseeded

Directions

a) Juice all the ingredients and mix thoroughly.

27. Ginger and fennel juice

Makes 2 servings

Ingredients

- 1 large fennel bulb
- 1cm (1/2in) cube fresh ginger root, peeled
- 2 celery stems
- 1/2 small cucumber
- 1/2 small green courgette
- 1 stem fresh basil

Directions

a) Juice all the ingredients, mix well, and drink immediately.

28. Fennel and broccoli sprouts juice

Makes 2 servings

Ingredients

- 1 large fennel bulb
- 45g (1 1/2oz) sprouted broccoli seeds
- 45g (1 1/2oz) sprouted alfalfa seeds
- 1 large carrot
- 2 stems celery
- 2-3 fresh mint leaves dash of lemon juice

Directions

a) Juice all the ingredients, add the lemon juice to taste, and mix well.

29.   Buckwheat greens and pea shoot juice

Makes 2 servings

Ingredients

- 2 Tablespoons young buckwheat greens, finely chopped
- 4 Tablespoons fresh pea shoots
- 2 courgettes
- 1 cucumber
- 2 Tablespoons fresh marjoram leaves
- a dash of lemon juice
- 200ml (7fl oz.) mineral water

Directions

a) Juice all ingredients, add the mineral water and lemon juice to taste, and mix well.

30.   Tomato salsa juice

Makes 2 servings

Ingredients

- 5 ripe tomatoes
- 1/2 cucumber
- 1 small clove of garlic
- 1/2 fresh red chilli, deseeded
- 1 stem fresh basil leaves
- 2 stems celery
- 1 teaspoons virgin olive oil
- salt to taste
- 1 red pepper, deseeded

Directions

a) Juice all the vegetables and herbs, add the olive oil, season to taste with a little salt if you wish, and mix well.

b) If you prefer your juice red, add 1 deseeded red pepper to the vegetables and herbs when you juice them.

31.   Artichoke leaf and fennel juice

Makes 2 servings

Ingredients

- 1 teaspoons artichoke leaves, finely chopped
- 1 medium fennel bulb
- 4 fresh dandelion leaves
- 4 celery stems
- 1/2 courgette

Directions

a) Juice all the ingredients, mix thoroughly, and drink.

b) If you find the juice overly bitter, dilute it with some mineral water until it tastes palatable.

32. Sunflower greens and wheatgrass juice

Makes 2 servings

Ingredients

- 100g (3 1/2oz) sunflower greens
- 100g (3 1/2oz) wheatgrass blades
- 300ml (10fl oz.) or more mineral water

Directions

a) Juice the sunflower greens and wheatgrass, blend well, and add enough mineral water to dilute the flavour of the juice and give it a palatable taste.

HERBAL TEAS

33. Lemon balm and rose tea

Makes 2-3 servings

Ingredients

- 16 leaves of fresh lemon balm (the soft flowering tops can also be used), or 1 Tablespoons dried lemon balm
- 2 rose heads with petals removed, or 2 Tablespoons dried rose petals

Directions

a) Put the fresh lemon balm leaves and rose petals in a large teapot. If using dried lemon balm and rose petals, spoon them into the teapot instead.

b) Boil 500ml (16fl oz.) of water, allow to cool for 5 minutes, then pour it into the teapot. Allow to infuse for 5 minutes and then serve. More water can be added later if needed to re-infuse the leaves and rose petals.

34. Jasmine and lemongrass tea

Makes 2 servings

Ingredients

- 1 stem lemongrass, chopped
- 1 Tablespoons jasmine flowers
- a dash of lime juice

Directions

a) Place the chopped lemongrass in a teapot and add the jasmine flowers.

b) Dilute 200ml (7fl oz.) of boiled water with 100ml (3/2fl oz.) of cold water so that the temperature of the hot water is approximately 70°C (158°F).

c) Pour the water into the teapot, allow the aroma to develop, and serve. In hot weather this tea can be served chilled.

35. Goji berry and damiana tea

Makes 2 servings

Ingredients

- 1 Tablespoons goji berries, fresh or dried
- 1 teaspoons damiana (Turnera diffusa)
- 1/2 teaspoons liquorice root powder

Directions

a) Place all the ingredients in a teapot, cover with 300ml (10fl oz.) of boiling water, allow to stand for 10-15 minutes, then serve. The infusion can also be left to cool and served as a cold drink.

36. Rosehip and bilberry tea

Makes 2 servings

Ingredients

- 1 Tablespoons rosehip shells, fresh or dried
- 1 Tablespoons bilberries, fresh or dried
- 1 teaspoon orange rind
- 1 teaspoon goji berries, fresh or dried

Directions

a) Place all ingredients in a teapot and cover with 300ml (10fl oz.) of boiling water.

b) Allow to infuse for 10-15 minutes, strain, and serve.

37. Chrysanthemum and elderflower tea

Makes 2 servings

Ingredients

- 1/2 Tablespoons chrysanthemum flowers
- 1/2 Tablespoons elderflowers
- 1/2 Tablespoons peppermint
- 1/2 Tablespoons nettle leaves

Directions

a) Place all the ingredients in a teapot, cover with 300ml (10fl oz.) of boiling water, allow to infuse, and serve.

b) Drink 3-4 cups a day during the hay fever season.

38. Chamomile and fennel tea

Makes 3 servings

Ingredients

- 1 teaspoon chamomile flowers
- 1 teaspoon fennel seeds
- 1 teaspoons meadowsweet
- 1 teaspoons marshmallow root, finely chopped
- 1 teaspoons yarrow

Directions

a) Put the herbs in a large teapot.

b) Boil 500ml (16fl oz.) of boiling water, and add to the teapot. Allow to infuse for 5 minutes and serve.

c) Drink 1 mug of the infusion 2-3 times a day.

39. Dandelion and burdock tea

Makes 3-4 servings

Ingredients

- 1 teaspoon dandelion leaves
- 1 teaspoon burdock leaves
- 1 teaspoons cleavers herb
- 1 teaspoon red clover flowers

Directions

a) Place all the ingredients in a teapot, pour in 500ml (16fl oz.) of boiling water, allow to infuse for 10-15 minutes, and serve. Drink hot or cold through the day.

40.   Yarrow and calendula tea

Makes 3-4 servings

Ingredients

- 1 teaspoons yarrow
- 1 teaspoon marigold flowers
- 1 teaspoons lady's mantle
- 1 teaspoons vervain
- 1 teaspoon raspberry leaf

Directions

a) Place all the ingredients in a teapot, pour in 500ml (16fl oz.) of boiling water, allow to infuse for 10-15 minutes, and serve. Drink hot or cold through the day.

b) Take 2-4 cups with the onset of pain, and reassess with your health professional if the pain persists.

41.   Skullcap and orange flower tea

Makes 3-4 servings

Ingredients

- 1 teaspoons skullcap
- 1 teaspoon orange flowers
- 1 teaspoons St. John's wort
- 1 teaspoons wood betony
- 1 teaspoons lemon balm

Directions

a) Place all the ingredients in a teapot, pour in 500ml (16fl oz.) of boiling water, allow to infuse for 10-15 minutes, and serve.

b) Drink hot or cold through the day.

42.   Blackberry and wild strawberry tea

Makes 3-4 servings

Ingredients

- 2 teaspoons blackberry leaves
- 1 teaspoon wild strawberry leaves
- 1 teaspoon raspberry leaves
- 1 teaspoon blackcurrant leaves

Directions

a) Place all the ingredients in a teapot, pour in 500ml (16fl oz.) of boiling water, allow to infuse for 10-15 minutes, and serve.

b) Drink hot or cold through the day.

43. Peppermint and calendula infusion

Makes 4 servings

Ingredients

- 1 teaspoon peppermint leaves
- 1 teaspoon calendula flowers
- 1 teaspoons motherwort
- 1 teaspoons vervain
- rose petal syrup to sweeten

Directions

a) Put all the herbs into a large teapot.

b) Boil 600ml (1 pint) of boiling water, and pour over the herbs. Allow to infuse for 20 minutes, then strain the liquid through a tea strainer into a clean jug. Drink 1 mug of the infusion 2-3 times a day, either hot or at room temperature.

44. Hawthorn flower and lavender tea

Makes 3-4 servings

Ingredients

- 1 teaspoon hawthorn flowers
- 1 teaspoons lavender
- 1 teaspoons rosebuds
- 1 teaspoon orange flowers
- 1 teaspoons jasmine

Directions

a) Place all the ingredients in a teapot, pour in 500ml (16fl oz.) of boiling water, allow to infuse for 10-15 minutes, and serve.

b) Drink hot or cold throughout the day.

45.   Nettle and cleavers tea

Makes 2 servings

Ingredients

- 2 teaspoons nettle leaves
- 2 teaspoons cleavers

Directions

a) Place the ingredients in a teapot, pour in 300ml (10fl oz.) of boiling water, allow to infuse for 10-15 minutes, and serve.

b) Drink hot or cold throughout the day.

46. Mullein and marshmallow tea

Makes 2 servings

Ingredients

- 1 teaspoon mullein leaves
- 1 teaspoon marshmallow leaves
- 1 teaspoons ribwort plantain

Directions

a) Place all the ingredients in a teapot, pour in 300ml (10fl oz.) of boiling water, allow to infuse for 10-15 minutes, and serve.

b) Drink hot or cold throughout the day.

47. Horsetail and cornsilk tea

Makes 5-6 servings

Ingredients

- 2 teaspoons horsetail
- 2 teaspoons corn silk
- 2 teaspoons dandelion leaves
- 2 teaspoons cleavers
- 2 teaspoons ribwort plantain leaves

Directions

a) Place all the ingredients in a teapot, pour in 600ml (1 pint) of boiling water, allow to infuse for 10-15 minutes, and serve.

b) Drink hot or cold throughout the day.

48. Fruited herbal iced tea

Yield: 1 serving

Ingredient

- 1 Bag Tazo Passion tea
- 1-quart Water
- 2 cups Fresh orange juice
- Orange wheel
- Mint leaves

Directions:

a) Place tea bag in 1 quart of boiling water and let steep for 5 minutes.

b) Remove tea bag. Pour tea into a 1-gallon pitcher filled with ice. Once the ice melts, fill the remaining space in the pitcher with water.

c) Fill a cocktail shaker with one half of brewed tea and one half orange juices. Shake well and strain into an ice filled tumbler glass. Garnish with orange wheel and mint leaves.

Yield: 1 serving

Ingredient

- Bag of dried lime flowers
- Boiling water

Directions:

a) Simply put dried flowers, one small handful to the average teapot, in the pot. Pour in the boiling water and stir well. Serve.

b) Do not allow steeping for longer than four minutes as the flavor will be lost.

49. **Raspberry herbal tea**

Yield: 8 servings

Ingredient

- 2 Family-size raspberry tea bags
- 2 Blackberry tea teabags
- 2 Black currant tea teabags
- 1 Bottle sparkling apple cider
- ½ cup Juice concentrate
- ½ cup Orange juice
- ½ cup Sugar

Directions:

a) Place all the Ingredients in a large pitcher. Chill. We serve ours with fruited ice cubes.

b) Reserve enough juices to fill an ice-cube tray and we place slices of strawberries and blueberries into each cube.

50.   Cardamom tea

Yield: 1 serving

Ingredient

- 15 Cardamom Seeds water
- ½ cup Milk
- 2 drops Vanilla (to 3 drops)
- Honey

Directions:

a) For indigestion, mix 15 pulverized seeds in ½ cup hot water. Add 1 ounce of fresh ginger root and a cinnamon stick.

b) Simmer 15 minutes over low heat. Add ½ cup milk and simmer 10 more minutes. Add 2 to 3 drops of vanilla. Sweeten with honey. Drink 1 to 2 cups daily.

51. Sassafras Tea

SERVES: 10

Ingredients

- 4 sassafras roots
- 2quarts water
- sugar or honey

Directions:

a) Wash roots and cut saplings off where they're green and where the root ends.

b) Bring water to a boil and add roots.

c) Simmer until the water is a deep brownish red (the darker the stronger -- I like mine strong).

d) Strain into a pitcher through wire and a coffee filter if you don't want any sediment.

e) Add honey or sugar to taste.

f) Serve hot or cold with lemon and a sprig of mint.

52.   Moringa Tea

Servings: 2

Ingredients

- 800 ml Water
- 5-6 Mint leaves - torn
- 1 teaspoon Cumin Seeds
- 2 teaspoon Moringa Powder
- 1 tablespoon Lime / Lemon Juice
- 1 teaspoon Organic Honey as sweetener

Directions:

a) Bring 4 cups of water to rolling boil.

b) Add 5-6 mint leaves and 1 teaspoon of cumin seeds / jeera.

c) Let it boil until water is reduced to half the quantity.

d) When water reduces to half, add 2 teaspoons of Moringa powder.

e) Regulate the heat to high, when it froths and comes up, turn off the heat.

f) Cover with a lid and let it sit for 4-5 minutes.

g) After 5 minutes, strain tea into a cup.

h) Add organic honey to taste and squeeze in fresh lime juice.

53.   Sage Tea

Ingredients

- 6 fresh sage leaves, left on stem
- Boiling water
- Honey (or agave syrup for vegan)
- 1 lemon wedge

Directions

a) Bring the water to a boil.

b) Wash the sage thoroughly.

c) Place the sage in a mug, and pour over the boiling water. Allow the herbs to steep for 5 minutes.

d) Remove the sage. Stir in a drizzle of honey and a squeeze of lemon.

CORDIALS AND SYRUPS

54.   Blackberry and lime cordial

Makes 500ml (16fl oz.)

Ingredients

- 1kg (2 1/4 lb) fresh blackberries juice of 4 limes
- 350g (12oz) caster sugar

Directions

a) Over a low heat, simmer the blackberries and lime juice in 600ml (1 pint) of water in a saucepan for approximately 15 minutes.

b) Leave to cool for 10 minutes or so, then push the mixture through a sieve and discard the pulp and pips. Pour the strained juice into a clean saucepan, and add the sugar. Stir over a low heat until the sugar has dissolved, and then simmer for about 5 minutes until the mixture is syrupy.

c) Pour into sterilized bottles, seal, refrigerate, and use within a few days. Dilute to taste with fizzy or still mineral water and fresh mint or lime slices to make a refreshing drink.

55.   Elderberry and elderflower cordial

Makes 500ml (16fl oz.)

Ingredients
- 50g (1 3/4oz) fresh or dried elderflowers
- 100g (3 1/2oz) elderberries
- 1 small cinnamon stick
- 1 teaspoons aniseed
- 1 Tablespoons fresh ginger root, grated
- 400g (14oz) sugar
- juice of 1/2 lemon

Directions

a) Place all the ingredients except the sugar and lemon juice in a saucepan, add 1 litre (1 3/4 pints) of water, cover, and simmer over a low heat for 25-30 minutes.

b) Strain the liquid into a measuring jar. Decant 600ml (1 pint) into a saucepan and add the sugar. (Any extra liquid can be drunk as tea.)

c) Stir gently over a low heat to dissolve the sugar. When all the sugar has dissolved, add the lemon juice and simmer gently for another 10-15 minutes with the lid off. Then bring it to the boil for 2-3 minutes and remove from the heat.

d) Pour into a sterilized glass bottle while still hot, seal, label with a list of the ingredients, and date. Keep refrigerated and use within 3-4 weeks.

e) Add a tablespoon of the cordial to a cup of cold or hot water, or drizzle on pancakes or breakfast cereals.

56.   Sweet violet and ginger honey

Makes 400–500g (14oz–1lb 2oz)

Ingredients

- 20g (3/4oz) fresh violet leaves and flowers (or use viola, or heartsease, if not available)
- 30g (1oz) fresh ginger root
- 20g (3/4oz) fresh plantain leaves
- 30g (1oz) fresh houttuynia leaves
- 500g (1lb 2oz) runny honey

Directions

a) Carefully harvest the fresh leaves and flowers and wash and air-dry them.

b) Finely chop them, place in a clean jar, and cover completely with runny honey. Mix thoroughly to ensure all the herbs are well covered. Add extra honey if necessary.

c) Leave in a warm place, such as an airing cabinet, for 5 days. Then strain the honey through a clean muslin cloth and decant it into a smaller sterilized jar.

d) Discard the strained herbs. 4 Seal the jar, label with a list of all the ingredients, and date.

57. Lemon balm and honey purée

Makes 125g (4 1/2oz)

Ingredients

- 20g (3/4oz) fresh lemon balm leaves
- 100g (3 1/2oz) runny honey
- Juice of 1/2 lemon

Directions

a) Place the leaves in a blender or food processor, add the honey and lemon juice, and blend until you get a smooth green purée. 2 Dilute with water and drink.

b) The purée will last for a week or two, if kept refrigerated.

58.   Rosehip syrup

Makes 700ml (1 1/4 pints)

Ingredients

- 500g (1lb 2oz) fresh rosehips
- 400g (14oz) sugar

Directions

a) Slice the fruit in half and scoop out the seeds and hairs with a small spoon. Wash the cleaned halves under running water to further remove the little hairs from the fruit.

b) Place the fruit in a saucepan, add 600ml (1 pint) of water, and simmer, uncovered, over a low heat for 20-30 minutes until the fruit is soft and the water has reduced slightly.

c) Strain the mixture and decant the liquid into a clean saucepan. Discard the fruit. Add the sugar to the strained liquid and allow it to dissolve over a low heat, stirring constantly.

d) Once all the sugar has dissolved, increase the heat and boil for 2-3 minutes. Decant the syrup into a sterilized bottle.

59. Mullein and aniseed syrup

Makes 200ml (7fl oz.)

Ingredients

- 4 teaspoons mullein leaf tincture
- 4 teaspoons marshmallow root tincture
- 1 Tablespoons aniseed tincture
- 1 Tablespoons thyme tincture
- 4 teaspoons plantain tincture
- 2 teaspoons liquorice root tincture 100ml (3 1/2 fl oz.) manuka honey

Directions

a) Blend the tinctures and honey, mix thoroughly, and pour into a sterilized brown glass bottle. Seal, label with all the ingredients, and date.

b) It will keep for 3-4 months.

60.   Rose petal syrup

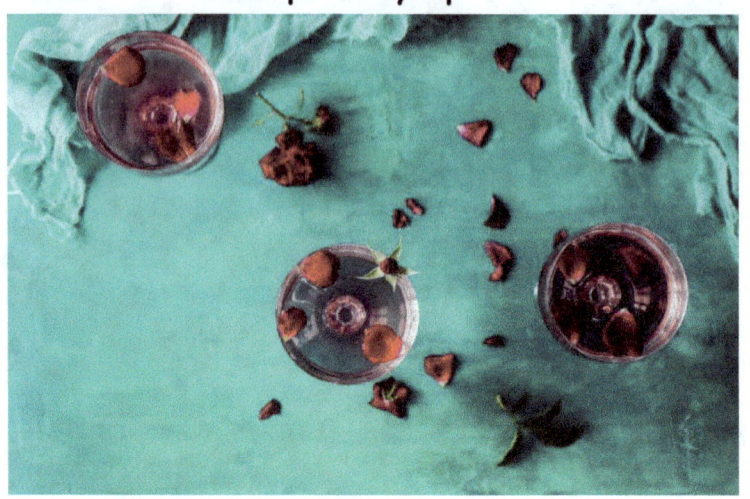

Makes approximately 500ml (16fl oz.)

Ingredients

- 225g (8oz) granulated sugar juice of 1 lemon, strained juice of 1 orange, strained
- 100g (3 1/2 oz) dried rose petals or
- 10 fresh rose heads

Directions

a) Dissolve the sugar in 300ml (10fl oz.) of water in a small saucepan over a low heat, and do not allow it to boil, as this will make the mixture cloudy. Add the strained lemon and orange juices, turn the heat down and simmer over a low heat for 5 minutes.

b) Over the next 15 minutes, add the rose petals, a tablespoon at a time, and stir thoroughly before adding more. Remove from the heat, allow to cool, and strain. Pour into a sterilized glass bottle, seal, and label. Keep refrigerated and use within 6 weeks.

61. Sour cherry syrup

Makes 1 pint

Ingredients

- 400ml (14fl oz.) sour cherry juice, freshly pressed
- 250g (9oz) sugar

Directions

a) Pour the juice into a saucepan, add the sugar, and heat gently. Dissolve the sugar in the juice, stirring constantly, then simmer for 20 minutes on a low heat.

b) Strain the syrup and bottle in a sterilized glass bottle with a tight-fitting lid. Keep refrigerated and use within a few weeks.

c) Drink diluted with cold or hot mineral water.

62.   Echinacea and thyme syrup

Makes 500ml (16fl oz.)

Ingredients

- 20g (¾oz) fresh thyme
- 20g (¾oz) fresh ribwort plantain leaves
- 20g (¾oz) fresh echinacea root, stem, and green leaves
- 10g (1/4oz) fresh ginger root, grated
- 10g (1/4oz) fresh garlic, skinned and crushed
- 10g (1/4oz) fresh elecampane root
- 1 whole fresh red chilli, finely chopped
- 400ml (14fl oz.) good-quality vodka
- 100g (31/2oz) manuka honey

Directions

a) Wash all the herb ingredients once they have been harvested and allow to dry. Then chop them finely.

b) Place all the ingredients except the honey and vodka in a large glass jar with a lid. Pour in the vodka, close the lid tightly, and shake a few times. Label the jar with the ingredients and the date. Place the jar in a dark cupboard and shake it at least once a day for 3 weeks.

c) Strain the contents of the jar through the muslin bag into a measuring jug. Decant the manuka honey into a bowl and gently pour in the tincture, stirring continuously with a whisk until the honey and tincture are well blended. Pour the syrup into a 500ml (16fl oz.) amber glass bottle with a lid, and label with the ingredients and the original starting date.

d) Take 1 teaspoon 2-3 times a day, or up to 6 teaspoons a day at the onset of a cold. This syrup should keep for up to 9 months.

HERBAL TINCTURES

63. Peppermint and thyme tincture

Makes 500ml (16fl oz.)

Directions

a) Place all the ingredients except the vodka in a large jar.

b) Cover with the vodka, stir, and make sure all the ingredients are well immersed. Seal the jar tightly and place it in a dark cupboard. Give the jar a few good shakes every day for 3 weeks.

c) Open the jar and strain the ingredients through a muslin-lined sieve into a shallow bowl. Discard the ingredients in the muslin and pour the liquid into an amber glass bottle. Label the tincture bottle with the names of all the ingredients and the date. Take 1 teaspoon in a glass of warm or cold water and sip before or after meals.

64. Elderberry and liquorice tincture

Makes 300–350ml (10–12fl oz.)

Ingredients

- 25g (scant 1oz) elderberries
- 25g (scant 1oz) echinacea root
- 10g (1/4oz) liquorice root
- 10g (1/4oz) fresh ginger root, grated
- 10g (1/4oz) cinnamon stick, broken into small pieces
- 20g (3/4oz) peppermint
- 400ml (14fl oz.) good-quality vodka

Directions

a) Ensure that all the dried ingredients are finely chopped, but not powdered.

b) Place all the ingredients except the vodka into a large glass jar with a secure-fitting lid. Pour in the vodka, close the lid tightly, and shake a few times.

c) Label the jar with all the ingredients and the date. Place the jar in a dark cupboard and shake it at least once every day for 3 weeks.

d) Strain the contents of the jar through a muslin bag into a measuring jug and pour the tincture into an appropriately sized (350–400ml/12–14fl oz.) sterilized amber glass bottle.

e) Seal the bottle.

f) Label with all the ingredients and the original starting date. Start by taking a few drops each day and build up to 1 teaspoon 2–3 times a day. Use within 6 months.

65. Lime flower and hawthorn berry tincture

Makes 300–350ml (10–12fl oz.)

Ingredients

- 20g (3/4oz) lime flowers
- 20g (3/4oz) hawthorn berries
- 20g (3/4oz) yarrow
- 20g (3/4oz) lemon balm
- 20g (3/4oz) crampbark
- 400ml (14fl oz.) good-quality vodka

Directions

a) Ensure that all the dried ingredients are finely chopped, but not powdered.

b) Place all the ingredients except the vodka into a large glass jar with a secure-fitting lid. Pour in the vodka, close the lid tightly, and shake a few times.

c) Label the jar with all the ingredients and the date. Place the jar in a dark cupboard and shake it at least once every day for 3 weeks.

d) Strain the contents of the jar through a muslin bag into a measuring jug and pour the tincture into an appropriately sized (350–400ml/12–14fl oz.) sterilized amber glass bottle. Seal the bottle.

e) Label with all the ingredients and the original starting date. Start by taking a few drops each day and build up to 1 teaspoon 2–3 times a day. Use within 6 months.

66. Passionflower and chamomile tincture

Makes 300–350ml (10–12fl oz.)

Ingredients

- 20g (3/4oz) passionflower
- 20g (3/4oz) chamomile
- 20g (3/4oz) valerian root
- 30g (1oz) sour cherries, fresh or dried 400ml (14fl oz.) good-quality vodka

Directions

a) Ensure that all the dried ingredients are finely chopped, but not powdered.

b) Place all the ingredients except the vodka into a large glass jar with a secure-fitting lid. Pour in the vodka, close the lid tightly, and shake a few times.

c) Label the jar with all the ingredients and the date. Place the jar in a dark cupboard and shake it at least once every day for 3 weeks.

d) Strain the contents of the jar through a muslin bag into a measuring jug and pour the tincture into an appropriately sized (350–400ml/12–14fl oz.) sterilized amber glass bottle.

e) Seal the bottle.

f) Label with all the ingredients and the original starting date. Start by taking a few drops each day and build up to 1 teaspoon in the late afternoon and another before going to bed. Use within 6 months.

67.   Chaste berry and dang gui tincture

Makes 300–350ml (10–12fl oz.)

Ingredients

- 20g (3/4oz) chaste berry (also called agnus castus)
- 20g (3/4oz) Chinese angelica (dang gui)
- 20g (3/4oz) motherwort
- 20g (3/4oz) black haw root bark (Viburnum prunifolium)
- 20g (3/4oz) chamomile
- 400ml (14fl oz.) good-quality vodka

Directions

a) Ensure that all the dried ingredients are finely chopped, but not powdered.

b) Place all the ingredients except the vodka into a large glass jar with a secure-fitting lid. Pour in the vodka, close the lid tightly, and shake a few times.

c) Label the jar with all the ingredients and the date. Place the jar in a dark cupboard and shake it at least once every day for 3 weeks.

d) Strain the contents of the jar through a muslin bag into a measuring jug and pour the tincture into an appropriately sized (350–400ml/12–14fl oz.) sterilized amber glass bottle. Seal the bottle.

e) Label with all the ingredients and the original starting date. Start by taking a few drops each day and build up to 1 teaspoon 2–3 times a day. Use within 6 months.

68.   Goji berry and Siberian ginseng tincture

Makes 300–350ml (10–12fl oz.)

Ingredients

- 25g (scant 1oz) goji berries
- 25g (scant 1oz) Siberian ginseng
- 25g (scant 1oz) oat tops or dried oats
- 20g (3/4oz) schisandra berries
- 5g (1/8oz) liquorice root
- 400ml (14fl oz.) good-quality vodka

Directions

a) Ensure that all the dried ingredients are finely chopped, but not powdered.

b) Place all the ingredients except the vodka into a large glass jar with a secure-fitting lid. Pour in the vodka, close the lid tightly, and shake a few times.

c) Label the jar with all the ingredients and the date. Place the jar in a dark cupboard and shake it at least once every day for 3 weeks.

d) Strain the contents of the jar through a muslin bag into a measuring jug and pour the tincture into an appropriately sized (350-400ml/12-14fl oz.) sterilized amber glass bottle. Seal the bottle.

e) Label with all the ingredients and the original starting date. Start by taking a few drops each day and build up to 1 teaspoon 2-3 times a day. Use within 6 months.

69. Red clover and cleavers tincture

Makes 300–350ml (10–12fl oz.)

Ingredients

- 15g (1/2oz) red clover
- 15g (1/2oz) cleavers
- 20g (3/4oz) viola (heartsease)
- 20g (3/4oz) violet leaves (Viola odorata)
- 20g (3/4oz) mahonia root (Mahonia aquifolium), finely chopped
- 20g (3/4oz) gotu kola
- 400ml (14fl oz.) good-quality vodka

Directions

a) Ensure that all the dried ingredients are finely chopped, but not powdered.

b) Place all the ingredients except the vodka into a large glass jar with a secure-fitting lid. Pour in the vodka, close the lid tightly, and shake a few times.

c) Label the jar with all the ingredients and the date. Place the jar in a dark cupboard and shake it at least once every day for 3 weeks.

d) Strain the contents of the jar through a muslin bag into a measuring jug and pour the tincture into an appropriately sized (350-400ml/12-14fl oz.) sterilized amber glass bottle. Seal the bottle.

e) Label with all the ingredients and the original starting date. Start by taking a few drops each day and build up to 1 teaspoon 2-3 times a day. Use within 6 months.

70. Echinacea and elderberry winter guard tincture

Makes 1 month's supply

Ingredients

- 20g (3/4oz) fresh ginger root
- 80g (23/4oz) echinacea root, fresh or dried
- 20g (3/4oz) thyme leaves, fresh or dried
- 2 garlic cloves (optional)
- 1 fresh chilli with seeds (optional)
- 80g (23/4oz) elderberries, fresh or dried
- 500ml (16fl oz.) good-quality vodka

Directions

a) Slice the fresh ginger and echinacea root thinly, pull the fresh thyme leaves from their stems, and mince the garlic and chilli (if using them).

b) Gently squeeze the elderberries. Place all the ingredients in a large jar with a securely fitting lid. Cover with the vodka, mix thoroughly, and make sure all the ingredients are completely immersed.

c) Close the top tightly and place the jar in a dark cupboard. Check it every day, shaking the jar a few times. After 3 weeks, open the jar, strain the ingredients through a muslin bag, collect the liquid in a sterilized amber glass bottle, label with the names of all the ingredients, and date.

71.   Dandelion and burdock tincture

Makes 300–350ml (10–12fl oz.)

Ingredients

- 20g (3/4oz) dandelion root
- 20g (3/4oz) burdock root
- 20g (3/4oz) schisandra berries
- 10g (1/4oz) artichoke leaves
- 20g (3/4oz) milk thistle
- 10g (1/4oz) gentian root
- 400ml (14fl oz.) good-quality vodka

Directions

a) Ensure that all the dried ingredients are finely chopped, but not powdered.

b) Place all the ingredients except the vodka into a large glass jar with a secure-fitting lid. Pour in the vodka, close the lid tightly, and shake a few times.

c) Label the jar with all the ingredients and the date. Place the jar in a dark cupboard and shake it at least once every day for 3 weeks.

d) Strain the contents of the jar through a muslin bag into a measuring jug and pour the tincture into an appropriately sized (350-400ml/12-14fl oz.) sterilized amber glass bottle.

e) Seal the bottle.

f) Label with all the ingredients and the original starting date. Start by taking a few drops each day and build up to 1 teaspoon 2-3 times a day. Use within 6 months.

72. Crampbark and valerian tincture

Makes 300–350ml (10–12fl oz.)

Ingredients

- 25g (scant 1oz) crampbark
- 25g (scant 1oz) valerian root
- 20g (3/4oz) passionflower
- 20g (3/4oz) chamomile
- 400ml (14fl oz.) good-quality vodka

Directions

a) Ensure that all the dried ingredients are finely chopped, but not powdered.

b) Place all the ingredients except the vodka into a large glass jar with a secure-fitting lid. Pour in the vodka, close the lid tightly, and shake a few times.

c) Label the jar with all the ingredients and the date. Place the jar in a dark cupboard and shake it at least once every day for 3 weeks.

d) Strain the contents of the jar through a muslin bag into a measuring jug and pour the tincture into an appropriately sized (350-400ml/12-14fl oz.) sterilized amber glass bottle. Seal the bottle.

e) Label with all the ingredients and the original starting date. Start by taking a few drops each day and build up to 1 teaspoon 2-3 times a day. Use within 6 months.

73.   Black cohosh and sage tincture

Makes 300–350ml (10–12fl oz.)

Ingredients
- 20g (3/4oz) black cohosh root
- 15g (1/2oz) chaste berry
- 10g (1/4oz) sage
- 20g (3/4oz) schisandra berries
- 15g (1/2oz) motherwort
- 20g (3/4oz) skullcap
- 400ml (14fl oz.) good-quality vodka

Directions

a) Ensure that all the dried ingredients are finely chopped, but not powdered.

b) Place all the ingredients except the vodka into a large glass jar with a secure-fitting lid. Pour in the vodka, close the lid tightly, and shake a few times.

c) Label the jar with all the ingredients and the date. Place the jar in a dark cupboard and shake it at least once every day for 3 weeks.

d) Strain the contents of the jar through a muslin bag into a measuring jug and pour the tincture into an appropriately sized (350–400ml/12–14fl oz.) sterilized amber glass bottle. Seal the bottle.

e) Label with all the ingredients and the original starting date. Start by taking a few drops each day and build up to 1 teaspoon 2–3 times a day. Use within 6 months.

74. Birch leaf and nettle root tincture

Makes 300–350ml (10–12fl oz.)

Ingredients

- 25g (scant 1oz) nettle root
- 15g (1/2oz) birch leaves
- 25g (scant 1oz) pellitory-of-the-wall
- 15g (1/2oz) blackcurrant leaves
- 20g (3/4oz) white poplar, or poplar bark (Populus tremuloides)
- 400ml (14fl oz.) good-quality vodka

Directions

a) Ensure that all the dried ingredients are finely chopped, but not powdered.

b) Place all the ingredients except the vodka into a large glass jar with a secure-fitting lid. Pour in the vodka, close the lid tightly, and shake a few times.

c) Label the jar with all the ingredients and the date. Place the jar in a dark cupboard and shake it at least once every day for 3 weeks.

d) Strain the contents of the jar through a muslin bag into a measuring jug and pour the tincture into an appropriately sized (350–400ml/12–14fl oz.) sterilized amber glass bottle. Seal the bottle.

e) Label with all the ingredients and the original starting date. Start by taking a few drops each day and build up to 1 teaspoon 2–3 times a day. Use within 6 months.

HERBAL FOODS

75. Crumbled herbal chicken

Yield: 2 serving

Ingredient

- 2 cups Bread crumbs
- 1 teaspoon Salt
- 1 teaspoon Freshly ground pepper
- 2 tablespoons Dried parsley
- 1 teaspoon Dried marjoram
- 1 teaspoon Dried thyme
- 1 teaspoon Dried oregano
- 1 teaspoon Garlic powder
- 1 Orange; sliced
- 4 Chicken breast halves boned and skinned
- 2 Eggs; beaten OR Egg substitute
- 2 tablespoons Butter or margarine
- 2 tablespoons Vegetable oil
- 1 cup Chicken stock or white wine
- 1 Sprig fresh parsley

Directions:

a) Place bread crumbs, salt, pepper, parsley, marjoram, thyme, oregano, and garlic powder in a food processor and grind thoroughly. Dip the chicken breasts into the beaten egg and then coat with bread crumbs.

b) Over medium-high heat, brown the chicken breasts on both sides in butter and oil. Lower the heat, add stock or wine, and cover. Simmer for 20 to 30 minutes, depending on the thickness of the breasts.

c) Garnish with orange slices and parsley.

76.   Cream of chicken with herbs

Yield: 1 serving

Ingredient

- 1 can Cream of Chicken Soup
- 1 can Chicken Broth
- 1 can Milk
- 1 can Water
- 2 cups Bisquick Baking Mix
- $\frac{3}{4}$ cup Milk

Directions:

a) Empty cans of soup into large pan

b) Stir in cans of water and milk. Mix together till smooth. Heat on medium heat until boiling

c) Stir together Bisquick and milk. Dough should be thick and sticky. Drop dough by teaspoonful into boiling soup.

d) Cook dumplings for approx. 8 to 10 minutes. uncovered

77.   Apricot Dijon glazed turkey

Yield: 6 serving

Ingredient

- 6 Chicken bouillon cubes
- 1½ cup Uncooked long-grain white rice
- ½ cup Slivered almonds
- ½ cup Chopped dried apricots
- 4 Green onions with tops; sliced
- ¼ cup Snipped fresh parsley
- 1 tablespoon Orange zest
- 1 teaspoon Dried rosemary; crushed
- 1 teaspoon Dried thyme leaves
- 1 Boneless turkey breast half -about 2 1/2 pounds
- 1 cup Apricot jam or orange marmalade
- 2 tablespoons Dijon mustard

Directions:

a) For herbed pilaf, bring water to a boil. Add bouillon. Remove from heat to a bowl. Add all remaining pilaf Ingredients except turkey; mix well. Place Turkey on top of rice mixture.

b) Cover and Bake 45 minutes

c) Remove turkey from oven; carefully remove Baker with Oven Mitts.

d) Stir pilaf just before serving, serve with turkey and sauce.

78.   Chicken and rice on herb sauce

Yield: 4 serving

Ingredient

- ¾ cup Hot water
- ¼ cup White wine
- 1 teaspoon Chicken flavored bouillon granules
- 4 (4 oz.) chicken breast halves skinned and boned
- ½ teaspoon Cornstarch
- 1 tablespoon Water
- 1 pack Neufchatel-style cheese with herbs and spices
- 2 cups Hot cooked long grain rice

Directions:

a) Bring hot water, wine and bouillon granules to a boil in large skillet over medium-high heat. Reduce heat and add chicken, simmer 15 minutes; turning after 8 minutes. Remove chicken when done, keep warm. Bring cooking liquid to boil, reduce to ⅔ cup.

b) Combine cornstarch and water and add to liquid. Bring to boil and cook 1 minute, stirring constantly. Add cream cheese and cook until well blended, stirring constantly with wire whisk. To serve:

c) Top rice with chicken, spoon sauce over chicken

79.   Chicken in cream and herb

Yield: 6 serving

Ingredient

- 6 Chicken thighs, skinned and boned
- All-purpose flour seasoned with salt and pepper
- 3 tablespoons Butter
- 3 tablespoons Olive oil
- ½ cup Dry white wine
- 1 tablespoon Lemon juice
- ½ cup Whipping cream
- ½ teaspoon Dried thyme
- 2 tablespoons Minced fresh parsley
- 1 Lemon, sliced (garnish)
- 1 tablespoon Capers, rinsed and drained (garnish)

Directions:

a) In a large skillet, heat 1½ tablespoons each butter and oil. Add pieces of chicken as will fit without crowding. Cook

b) Add wine and lemon juice to skillet and simmer over moderately high heat, stirring to blend in browned particles. Boil, reducing to about half

c) Add whipping cream, thyme, and parsley; boil until sauce thickens slightly. Pour any meat juices from warming platter into sauce.

d) Adjust sauce for seasoning to taste. Pour over meat and garnish with parsley, lemon slices and capers

80. Chicken madeira on biscuits

Yield: 6 serving

Ingredient

- 1½ pounds Chicken breast
- 1 tablespoon Cooking oil
- 2 Cloves garlic, minced
- 4½ cup Quartered fresh mushrooms
- ½ cup Chopped onion
- 1 cup sour cream
- 2 tablespoons All-purpose flour
- 1 cup Skim milk
- ½ cup Chicken broth
- 2 tablespoons Madeira or dry sherry

Directions:

a) Cook chicken in hot oil over medium-high heat for 4 - 5 minutes or till no longer pink. Add garlic, mushrooms and onion to skillet. Cook, uncovered, for 4 - 5 minutes or till liquid evaporates.

b) In a bowl stir together sour cream, flour, ½ teaspoon salt and ¼ teaspoon pepper. Add sour cream mixture, milk, and broth to skillet. Add chicken and Madeira or sherry; heat through.

c) Serve over Herbed Biscuits.

81. Chicken soup with herbs

Yield: 7 serving

Ingredient

- 1 cup Dried cannellini beans
- 1 teaspoon Olive oil
- 2 Leeks, trimmed -- washed
- 2 Carrots -- peeled and diced
- 10 milliliters Garlic -- finely chopped
- 6 Plum tomatoes
- 6 New potatoes
- 8 cups Home-made Chicken Broth
- ¾ cup Dry white whine
- 1 Sprig fresh thyme
- 1 Sprig fresh rosemary
- 1 Bay leaf

Directions:

a) Rinse beans and pick over, cover with water and set aside to soak for 8 hours or overnight. In a large pot, heat oil over medium-low heat. Add leeks, carrots and garlic; cook until softened, about 5 minutes. Stir in tomatoes and cook for 5 minutes. Add potatoes and cook for 5 minutes.

b) Add chicken broth, wine and herbs; bring to a boil. Drain the beans and add to the pot; cook 2 hours, or until the beans are soft.

c) Remove the bay leaf and herb sprigs before serving.

82. Chicken with wine and herbs

Yield: 4 serving

Ingredient

- Frying chicken
- $\frac{1}{2}$ teaspoon Oregano
- $\frac{1}{2}$ teaspoon Basil
- 1 cup Dry white wine
- $\frac{1}{2}$ teaspoon Garlic salt
- $\frac{1}{2}$ teaspoon Salt
- $\frac{1}{4}$ teaspoon Pepper

Directions:

a) Wash chicken and cut up. In small amount of Oil, brown chicken pieces on all sides. Pour off excess Oil.

b) Add Wine and seasoning and simmer for 30 to 40 minutes or until chicken is tender.

83.   Herbal ravioli

Ingredient

- 2 8.5x11" fresh pasta sheets
- 1¼ cup Ricotta cheese; fat free
- ¾ cup Italian bread crumbs
- ¼ cup Fresh basil and ¼ cup Fresh parsley; chopped
- ⅛ teaspoon oreganoo and ⅛ Nutmeg
- Salt and Black pepper
- Poached tomato base
- 2 large Tomatoes; ripe
- 2 Cloves garlic; thinly sliced
- 6 Fresh basil leaves

Directions:

a) In large mixing bowl, combine ricotta, bread crumbs, basil, parsley, oregano, nutmeg, salt and black pepper.

b) Lay pasta sheets flat on work surface and drop four equal portions (about ¼ cup) of ricotta mixture onto the 4 quadrants on the left half only of each sheet of pasta. Fold right half of pasta sheet over other half. Press down around each cheese mound to seal.

c) Bring water to boil in large pot. Drop ravioli into water and boil 3-5 minutes. Wash, core, peel and rough-chop tomatoes. Set aside. Briefly sauté garlic, Add tomatoes, basil, water and salt

d) Cover and cook 5 minutes. Spoon tomato mixture onto 4 serving plates and top each plate with two raviolis.

84. Linguine with mixed herb

Yield: 1 serving

Ingredient

- 4 mediums Carrots
- 3 mediums Zucchini
- 1 pounds Dried linguine
- 1 cup Packed fresh flat-leafed parsley leaves
- ½ cup Packed fresh basil leaves
- 1 tablespoon Fresh thyme leaves
- 1 tablespoon Fresh rosemary leaves
- 1 tablespoon Fresh tarragon leaves
- ½ cup Freshly grated Parmesan
- ⅓ cup Olive oil
- ¼ cup Walnuts; toasted golden
- 1 tablespoon Balsamic vinegar

Directions:

a) In a 6-quart kettle bring 5 quarts salted water to a boil. Add linguine and cook 8 minutes, or until barely tender. Add carrots and cook 1 minute. Add zucchini and cook 1 minute. Reserve ⅔ cup cooking water and drain pasta and vegetables.

b) In a large bowl stir together pesto and reserved hot cooking water. Add pasta and vegetables and toss well.

c) In a food processor blend together all Ingredients with salt and pepper to taste until smooth.

85. Farfalle with herb sauce

Yield: 1 serving

Ingredient

- 2 cloves garlic -- minced
- 1 lb. farfalle -- cooked
- 2 c fresh mint sprigs
- $\frac{3}{4}$ extra virgin olive oil
- $\frac{1}{2}$ c vegetable stock
- $1\frac{1}{2}$ teaspoons salt
- $\frac{1}{2}$ teaspoons fresh pepper
- 1 Tablespoons lemon juice
- $\frac{1}{2}$ c walnuts, toasted, chopped
- $\frac{1}{2}$ c Parmesan cheese

Directions:

a) In a blender, or food processor, add the herbs and garlic, and while the machine is running, drizzle in $\frac{1}{2}$ olive oil, the vegetable stock, and then the rest of the oil. Add salt, pepper and lemon, blend and taste and adjust seasoning.

b) Toss with cooked pasta while still warm, fold in nuts and cheese. Garnish with fresh herb sprigs.

86. Egg noodles with garlic

Yield: 4 serving

Ingredient

- ½ pounds Egg noodles
- 4 large Garlic clove(s)
- 1½ cup Mixed herbs
- 2 tablespoons Extra-virgin olive oil
- Salt and pepper

Directions:

a) Cook the pasta in a large pot of boiling, salted water until tender but still firm, 7-9 minutes. Drain well.

b) Meanwhile, chop the garlic, Mince the herbs; you'll have about 1 cup.

c) Combine the olive oil and garlic in a large frying pan. Cook over medium heat, stirring occasionally, until the garlic is fragrant but not browned, 2-3 minutes. Remove from the heat and stir in the minced herbs.

d) Add the cooked noodles to the frying pan and toss. Season with salt and pepper to taste and toss well

87. Cappelini with herb spinach

Yield: 6 serving

Ingredient

- 8 ounces Angel hair pasta(cappelini)
- 10 ounces frozen spinach
- 1 pounds Fresh spinach
- 1 tablespoon Virgin olive
- 1 Onion; chopped
- 2 tablespoons Fresh parsley
- $\frac{1}{2}$ teaspoon Dried leaf basil
- $\frac{1}{2}$ teaspoon Dried leaf oregano
- $\frac{1}{2}$ teaspoon Ground nutmeg
- Salt and pepper to taste
- 2 tablespoons Grated Parmesan cheese;

Directions:

a) Bring a large kettle of water to a boil and cook pasta until al dente, 3 minutes. Drain in a colander; set aside. Meanwhile place frozen spinach in a steamer rack over boiling water until slightly wilted.

b) In a non-stick skillet, heat oil and Sauté onion until softened. Place spinach, onion, parsley, basil, oregano, nutmeg, salt and pepper in a blender of a food processor fitted with metal blade, and process to purée. Place pasta in a serving bowl, toss with sauce and sprinkle with Parmesan cheese

88. Malaysian herbal rice

Ingredient

- 400 grams' Fresh salmon
- 2 tablespoons soy sauce and 2 tablespoons Mirin
- 6 cups Cooked jasmine rice
- Kaffir lime leaves
- ½ cup Toasted; shredded coconut
- Turmeric/galangal; peeled
- 3 tablespoons Fish sauce

Dressing

- 2 smalls Red chilies; seeded and minced
- ½ cup Thai basil
- ½ cup Vietnamese mint
- 1 Ripe avocado; peeled
- 1 Red chilli; minced
- 2 Cloves garlic; minced
- ⅓ cup Lime juice

Directions:

a) Mix the soy and mirin and pour over the fish and marinate for 30 minutes. Heat a grill pan or griller then cook the fish until golden.

b) Julienne the turmeric, galangal, chilli and kaffir lime leaves and mix with the cooked rice. Add the toasted coconut, basil and mint and mix with the fish sauce. Set aside.

c) Purée all the dressing Ingredients, then fold the dressing through the rice until the rice is coloured pale green. Flake the cooked fish and add to the rice.

89.   Angel hair with smoked salmon

Yield: 4 serving

Ingredient

- 8 ounces Angel hair pasta; uncooked
- 6 ounces Smoked salmon; thinly sliced
- 3 tablespoons Olive oil
- 1 large Garlic; finely chopped
- $2\frac{1}{4}$ cup Chopped; seeded tomatoes
- $\frac{1}{2}$ cup Dry white wine
- 3 tablespoons Drained large capers
- $1\frac{1}{2}$ teaspoon Spice Islands Dill Weed
- $1\frac{1}{2}$ teaspoon Spice Islands Sweet Basil
- $\frac{1}{2}$ cup Parmesan cheese; freshly grated
- 2 cups tomatoes, wine

Directions:

a) Prepare pasta according to package directions.

b) Meanwhile, cut salmon, along the grain, into $\frac{1}{2}$-inch wide strips; set aside.

c) In large skillet, heat oil over medium-high heat until hot; cook and stir garlic until golden.

d) Stir capers, dill and basil; cook until mixture is hot, stirring occasionally.

e) In large bowl, combine pasta and tomato mixture; toss to combine.

f) Add salmon and cheese; toss lightly. Garnish with remaining tomatoes and parsley, if desired.

90. Codfish with herbs

Yield: 4 serving

Ingredient

- 3 cups Water
- $\frac{1}{2}$ cup Sliced celery
- 1 pack Instant chicken broth
- $\frac{1}{2}$ Lemon
- 2 tablespoons Dehydrated onion flakes
- 1 teaspoon Fresh parsley, chopped
- $\frac{1}{2}$ each Bay leaf
- $\frac{1}{8}$ teaspoon Ground cloves
- $\frac{1}{8}$ teaspoon Thyme
- 4 each boned and skinned cod steaks
- 2 mediums Tomatoes, cut in half
- 2 mediums Green peppers, seeded and cut in half

Directions:

a) In a 12-inch skillet, combine water, celery, broth mix, lemon, onion flakes, parsley, bay leaf, cloves and thyme. Bring to a boil, then reduce heat to a simmer. Add fish and poach 5 to 7 minutes. Add tomato and green pepper halves, and finish cooking until fish flakes easily. Remove fish and vegetables, keep warm.

b) Cook liquid until reduced by half. Remove lemon and bay leaf. Place liquid and half of the cooked tomato and peppers in a blender container. Purée until smooth

c) Pour over fish and remaining tomato and peppers.

91. Cold poached salmon

Yield: 1 serving

Ingredient

- 6 Skinless; (6ounce) salmon fillets
- Salt and white pepper
- 3 cups Fish stock or clam juice
- 1 bunch Oregano
- 1 bunch Basil
- 1 bunch Parsley
- 1 bunch Thyme
- 6 Tomatoes; peeled, seeded, and diced
- $\frac{1}{2}$ cup Extra virgin olive oil
- $1\frac{1}{2}$ teaspoon Salt
- $\frac{1}{2}$ teaspoon Freshly ground black pepper

Directions:

a) Season salmon all over with salt and pepper

b) Bring stock or juice to a boil in a large oven-proof skillet. Add fish, so they are barely touching, and bring liquid back to a boil. Transfer to oven and bake 5 minutes while turning fish over

c) To make dressing, remove stems and finely chop all herbs. Mix all Ingredients in a small bowl, and reserve in refrigerator.

92. Dill herb fillets

Yield: 4 serving

Ingredient

- 2 pounds' fillet of red snapper
- ¾ teaspoon salt
- ½ teaspoon ground pepper
- ½ cup olive oil
- 1½ tablespoon minced parsley
- 1 tablespoon minced shallots, spice
- 1 x hunter freeze dried or fresh
- 1 pinch oregano
- ¼ cup fresh squeezed lemon juice

Directions:

a) Arrange fish in a single layer, oiled, shallow baking dish. Sprinkle with oil, parsley, shallots, Dill Weed, and oregano. Bake in a preheated oven at 350 degrees F until flesh barely separates when tested with a fork--15 to 20 minutes. Baste twice with pan juices while baking. Remove fish to a serving dish.

b) Blend lemon juice into pan drippings, then pour over fish.

93.   Crispy baked fish and herbs

Yield: 4 serving

Ingredient

- 4 each Fillets white fish
- 1 tablespoon Water
- $\frac{1}{8}$ teaspoon Lemon pepper
- 1 teaspoon Low fat margarine, melted
- 1 each Egg white
- $\frac{1}{2}$ cup Cornflake crumbs
- 2 teaspoons Chopped fresh parsley

Directions:

a) Preheat oven 400F. Lightly spray a medium size shallow baking pan with vegetable spray. Rinse fish and pat dry.

b) In small bowl, beat egg white with a little water. Dip fish in egg white, then roll in crumbs. Arrange fish in baking pan. Sprinkle with lemon pepper and parsley, then drizzle margarine over all.

c) Bake uncovered 20 minutes or until fish flakes easily

94. Fettuccine with shrimp

Yield: 2 serving

Ingredient

- 1 pack Lipton creamy herb soup mix
- 8 ounces Shrimp
- 6 ounces Fettuccini, cooked
- $1\frac{3}{4}$ cup Milk
- $\frac{1}{2}$ cup Peas
- $\frac{1}{4}$ cup Parmesan, grated

Directions:

a) Mix soup mix with milk and bring to boiling. Add shrimp and peas and simmer 3 minutes until shrimp are tender.

b) Toss with hot noodles and cheese.

95. Mussels with garlic

Yield: 1 serving

Ingredient

- 1 kilograms Fresh live mussels
- 2 Shallots or 1 small onion
- 200 milliliters Dry white wine
- 1 Bay leaf
- 1 Sprig parsley
- 125 grams Butter
- 1 tablespoon Chopped parsley; up to 2
- 2 Cloves garlic; crushed
- Freshly ground black pepper
- 2 tablespoons Fresh white breadcrumbs to finish
- 250 grams Sea salt for presentation

Directions:

a) Chop the onion and place it in a good sized pan with the wine, bay leaf, thyme and parsley then bring them to simmering point. Add the mussels, checking that they are closed and discard any that are open.

b) Cover the pan and simmer for 5 or 6 minutes or until the mussels are open.

c) Beat the butter and thoroughly blend in the parsley and garlic with a little black pepper. Place 1/2 teaspoons on each mussel, add a light sprinkling of breadcrumbs and place under a hot grill for 2-3 minutes.

Serve the mussels hot on the bed of sea salt.

96.   Fish Caribbean with wine

Yield: 1 serving

Ingredient

- 1 cup Rice or couscous -- cooked
- 4 Sheets parchment paper, foil
- 2 smalls Zucchini
- 1 Chile poblano
- Pasillo -- in thin strips
- 1 pounds Boneless firm white fish
- 4 mediums Tomatoes
- 10 Black olives
- 1 teaspoon Each chopped fresh basil
- Thyme -- tarragon
- Parsley, and green onion
- 1 Egg

Directions:

a) Place on a baking sheet and cook for 12 minutes or until fish is done! Place ½ cup of the cooked rice in the middle.

b) Top each serving with ½ cup of zucchini strips, a piece of the fish, ¼ cup diced tomato and 3 thin strips of the Chile.

c) Sprinkle a fourth of the chopped olives on each serving, and top with ¼ each of the fresh herbs.

d) Combine all the sauce Ingredients and purée. Pour into a small saucepan and bring to boil over medium heat. Strain

97.   Monkfish with garlicky herb

Yield: 4 serving

Ingredient

- 700 grams Filleted monkfish tails
- 85 grams Butter
- 2 Cloves garlic -- crushed
- Egg (beaten)
- Juice of one lemon
- 1 teaspoon Finely chopped herbs
- Seasoned flour

Directions:

a) Soften butter and add herbs and garlic. Chill. -- Make a slit in each Monkfish fillet and pack with the chilled herb butter. Fold up to enclose butter. Toss each piece in seasoned flour, dip in beaten egg and roll in breadcrumbs. Press the crumbs firmly onto the fish.

b) Place the fish in a buttered dish. Dribble a little melted butter or oil, and lemon juice, on top. Cook for 30-35 minutes at 375F/190C.

c) Serve at once.

98. Herbed pork cutlets

Yield: 4 serving

Ingredient

- 1 Egg
- ⅓ cup Dry bread crumbs
- ¼ cup Fresh basil, chopped
- 2 tablespoons Fresh oregano, chopped
- 1 tablespoon Parmesan, fresh grated
- 1 teaspoon Fresh thyme, chopped
- ½ teaspoon Pepper
- ¼ teaspoon Salt
- 1 pounds Fast-fry pork cutlets
- 2 tablespoons Vegetable oil

Directions:

a) In shallow dish, lightly beat egg. In separate shallow dish, stir together bread crumbs, basil, oregano, Parmesan, thyme, pepper and salt. Dip pork into egg to coat well; press into bread crumb mixture, turning to coat all over.

b) In large skillet, heat half of the oil. Over medium heat; cook pork, in batches and adding remaining oil if necessary, turning once, for 8-10 minutes or until just a hint of pink remains inside. Serve with new red potatoes and yellow beans.

99.   Monastery herbal sausage

Yield: 1 serving

Ingredient

- 400 grams Lean pork
- 400 grams Lean beef
- 200 grams' Green pork back fat or fatty
- Pork belly without skin
- 20 grams Salt
- 2 teaspoons finely ground White pepper
- 1 teaspoon Thyme
- 1 teaspoon Marjoram
- 5 Pieces pimento
- 1 Piece finely ground
- Cinnamon

Directions:

a) Mince pork, beef and fat through 8mm disc. Mix herbs and spices and sprinkle over meat mass and mix all together by hand for 5-10 minutes.

b) Fit funnel to mixer and fill pork casings. Twist into length of choice.

100. Fillet of lamb with herbs

Yield: 4 serving

Ingredient

- 450 grams Lamb neck fillet
- 1 teaspoon Dried thyme
- 1 teaspoon Dried rosemary
- 2 Cloves garlic, thinly sliced
- 2 tablespoons Olive oil
- Salt and freshly ground black pepper

Directions:

a) Cut each piece of lamb in half crossways then cut lengthways, not quite all the way through, and open out like a book. To cook safely on a barbecue, each piece should be no thicker than 2cm/ $\frac{3}{4}$ in. If it is any thicker, beat lightly with a rolling pin between 2 pieces of cling film

b) Combine all the remaining Ingredients in a bowl and add the lamb. Mix well, then cover and leave in the fridge for up to 48 hours, turning occasionally.

c) Place the meat on the barbecue grid and cook for 4-5 minutes each side.

d) Make sure it is thoroughly cooked. Brush lightly with the marinade during cooking.

CONCLUSION

Chefs and home cooks alike use fresh and dried herbs to make both sweet and savory dishes, ranging from rich sauces to light salads and herb-laced baked goods. In addition to their culinary uses, medicinal herbs and their valuable essential oils have been relied on for their health benefits since the Middle Ages, ranging from anti-inflammatory and antiviral benefits to skin-clearing topical powers.

Become a better herbal home cook with the dishes highlighted in this book.

www.ingramcontent.com/pod-product-compliance
Lightning Source LLC
Chambersburg PA
CBHW070659120526
44590CB00013BA/1028